KUMMTIBAA

The legendary cunning figure of the mishmi folktale

KATHESI KRI

Illustrator Diwanso Tamai

ISBN 979-8-89777-629-0

Contents

Acknowledgment

I sincerely thank my generous sponsor.

Smt. Dasanglu Pul

Hon'ble Minister,
Women & Child Development,
Cultural Affairs (Arts & Culture, Research, Gazetteers,
Science & Technology),
Govt. of Arunachal Pradesh.

her generous contributuons have played
a vital role in bringing this book to life.

Introduction

KUMMTIBAA THE LENGENDARY CUNNING FIGURE OF MISHMI FOLKTALE.

If you're from the Mishmi tribe, you've undoubtedly heard of Kummtibaa.

This iconic character has captivated children's imagination for generations. Mishmi ancestors often share tales of Kummtibaa to teach valuable moral lessons.

Whenever a child misbehaved or showed stubbornness. parents would caution 'Behave Or Khummtibaa will take you away!' This warning would instantly calm the child, demonstrating the power Of Khummtibaa's legend.

But who was Kummtibaa? Let me satisfy your curiosity.

Kummtibaa was a cunning and clever man. Kummtibaa wasn't originally from Mishmi community, our ancestors believe that, he was from Tibet [meyor] (Talong, as we say in our Mishmi language, meaning someone who is Tibetan).

According to our ancestors, he was driven out of his village for his cunning ways. Constant stealing breaking everyone's trust and more.

Kummtibaa, famous in Mishmi society was known for his unparalleled cleverness and mischievousness.

He was clever and cunning that he continued to deceive others even on his deathbed.

Dear Readers,

The story of Kummtibaa is not a direct reflection of Mishmi culture or traditions but rather a cherished tale in Mishmi community passed down through generations. It has been a widely told story among our ancestors used to impart lessons of morality and courage to young listeners.

Sadly in today's world stories like Kummtibaa are at risk of fading away. The influence of modern life has drawn us away from our traditional narratives and fewer and fewer Mishmi children grow up hearing these tales.

My purpose in writing this story is to preserve this fragment of our heritage to keep the spirit of Kummtibaa alive and to ensure that future generations can still learn from his story.

Chapter One

The Dead Body

Once upon a time, in a small village, a beloved grandma passed away. Relatives and the villagers gathered to pay their respects. Among them was Kummtibaa, a clever man with a sly look in his eye, who brought two fat hens.

As the mourners surrounded the deceased, Kummtibaa started to weave a story. "I felt something strange", he whispered to the family, "Grandma's spirit wants to eat my hens" The deceased's son angry replied, "How can a dead person eat? You're ridiculous, Kummtibaa!"

But Kummtibaa didn't give up. "I know it. Trust me," he insisted. Frustrated son challenged him, "Stay tonight, and we'll see if you're right. If not, leave and don't come back!" kummtibaa reply with a sly grin, "But if I'm not wrong, you owe me what i want." deceased's son accepted. kummtiibaa smiled innerly, sure his plan would work.

That night, Kummtibaa sneaked into the forest, killed his hens, ate its meat and placed the remains bones, feathers, and blood in the dead grandma's mouth.

An hour later, he shouted, "i told you, Grandma's spirit ate my hen!" The son and relatives were shocked, forced to admit Kummtibaa's cleverness.

Kummtibaa cunningly told the dead grandma's son, "Now you must fulfill your promise, you made a vow to me."

But the son, feeling deeply upset, replied that he had nothing to give, nor did he have any money. After thinking for a moment, kummtibaa demanded "I want grandma's body as payment"

The villagers gasped, "huh!" but the son keeping his word, agreed reluctantly. Kummtibaa felt victorious.

Next, Kummtibaa took the body to the swinging bridge, The bridge was a frequent crossing point for soldiers,enroute to other destinations. Therefore it was a busy spot for soldiers carrying valuable goods He dressed the deceased in clothes that made her look alive and sat her on the bridge's edge.

As soldiers rode across the swaying bridge, the motion caused the deceased's body to tumble he put on a dramatic act "Oh, Grandma, You fell ! How could you, cruel soldiers? "

Feeling guilty the soldiers gave

Kummtibaa chests filled with gold and jewels. With a pleased grin, Kummtibaa forgave them, grinning from ear to ear.

Chapter Two

The Tale of the Giant Rock

In the village of Yakung, nestled in Anjaw District, a massive rock loomed over the land, covering a significant portion of the area. The villagers struggled to cultivate their crops, often trekking far from home to find suitable farming and, accepting it as their fate.

Despite the rocky obstacles, yakung was a lively place, filled with greenery and bustling with domestic animals like pigs, hens, cows, and goats. One day, a greedy Kummtibaa wandered into the village. His eyes sparkled at the sight Of the animals, and he thought, What a feast this could be!

Kummtibaa approached the villagers with a sly grin. "Hey everyone," he began, "I see your struggles with farming. It pains me to watch you toil so far from home." He paused for effect, then continued his lies. "That giant rock over there is the problem. It blocks your good luck, prosperity and makes life hard for you all."

The villagers, stunned by his words, believed him.

"But don't worry," Kummtibaa added . "I have a solution. I can remove that giant rock and give you more land to cultivate."

The villagers, filled with hope rejoiced at his words.

"Thank you Kummtibaa," they exclaimed believing he was their savior.

But Kummtibaa, with a twinkle in his eye, added "I'll only help if you prepare a delicious feast for me like pork, chicken, whatever you have. I need energy for this enormous task."

Without hesitation, the villagers agreed, excited by the prospect of new farmland and a brighter future. Kummtibaa smiled wickedly, he had them right where he wanted them. He added one more condition "When I lift the rock, you must all push from behind and shout **Huisha**! **Huisha!** to give me strength!'

The next day, the villagers whipped up a grand feast. Kummtibaa devoured everything pork, chicken. He even fashioned a necklace from the leftover meat, feeling like a king as he led the villagers to the giant rock.

When they reached out to giant rock, Kummtibaa instructed everyone to gather behind the rock and push the giant rock shouting,

"Huisha! huisha!" The villagers cheered with enthusiasm chanting louder and louder, **"huisha! huisha!"**

But after much pushing, the rock didn't budge an inch! One curious villager peeked around the side and gasped! there was no Kummtibaa in sight. Instead, he found pig droppings where the cunning man had been. Kummtibaa had tricked them and vanished while they pushed in vain!

Realizing they had been deceived, the villagers felt a wave of sadness wash over them. They had lost their beloved animals and learned a hard lesson about greed and trust. All that was left was the giant rock and the bitter taste of regret.

Chapter Three
The salt scam.

The Salt Scam

The villagers were devastated by the trickery of the cunning kummtibaa, who had caused them to lose many of precious animals.

This left them furious and full of regret. Determined to punish Kummtibaa, they gathered together and chased after him.

kummtibaa, had tricked the villagers into pushing the enormous rock and was running away. Just then, One of the villagers saw Kummtibaa running far away from the village. "Hey, look! Where is he running off to?" SHOUTED pointing at him.

Kummtibaa, being as clever as ever, noticed the villagers closing in on him. Just in time, he spotted a deep underground cave hole nearby and jumped in to hide.

The villagers saw the kummtibaa's action therefore they quickly reached to the hole and wanting to find out how deep it was, they lowered a long thread.

Kummtibaa grinned slyly to himself. "Another fools" he thought.

He was confident because he knew that,

At that time, salt was a precious commodity, that was in short supply across all the villages, causing great concern among the villagers. They relied on salt not only for flavoring their food, but also for preserving it and without enough of it they worried about how they would sustain their families through the changing seasons.

Every day, the villagers gathered to discuss the salt shortage their faces filled with anxiety and uncertainty. They longed for a solution to this pressing problem wishing for ways to secure a steady supply of salt.

Aware about their misery, the cunning Kummtibaa thought to take advantage of it, hatched a plan to deceive them from under the cave hole.

Therefore, from inside the hole, he called out to the villagers. "Hey! Did you all know there's salt down here?" The villagers frowned. "Salt ! In this hole? That's impossible! You're lying, Kummtibaa!" "I'm not lying!" Kummtibaa insisted.

Kummtibaa continued "Alright, I'll prove there's salt down here! I'll smear some on this thread. Pull it up and taste it when I tell you." The innocent villagers curious and agreed. they lowered the thread.

Then Kummtibaa blew his nose, smearing sticky mucus all over it. With a mischievous twinkle in his eye, Kummtibaa shouted, "Pull it up now and taste it! You'll see it's salty!"

After a time, the villagers driven by curiosity, noticed something strange on the thread. Eager to uncover the mystery, they decided to taste it. To their surprise, the thread had a salty flavor!

The villagers were astonished. One of them exclaimed, "Oh, Kummtibaa must have reached the salt area!" The others nodded in amazement, Once again, they believed in

Kummtibaa's cunning plan. but the villagers were still furious, wanted to give punishment. Therefore the villagers

Waited and waited to get kummtibaa out, but kummtibaa didn't come out.

Frustrated and exhausted, the villagers came up with a new plan. They left behind a loud drum called a Madong, which could alert everyone, and set up a Mishmi-style trap weapon near the hole.

They assigned the oldest and most trusted villager, "the Chokidar" (watchman) to guard the hole.

They instructed, "if Kummtibaa tries to come out, sound the Madong so we can catch him!"

The Chokidar agreed and proudly took up h's post. But

Kummtibaa, ever the trickster, was already plotting his escape.

The Chokidar (watchman) followed the instructions Of villagers, but his curiosity made him tasted the thread again. TO his surprise, it really did taste salty! Excited, he exclaimed, "You're right! There's salt beneath our village!"

Kummtibaa chuckled to himself and said, "give me your hand, and I'll give you a lump of salt." Eager to get the precious salt, the Chokidar stretched out his hand into the hole. But the moment he did, SNAP! His hand got caught in the trap weapon the villagers had set for Kummtibaa! "Aiyaaah!" he cried, stuck and helpless.

The Kummtibaa didn't waste a second. He scrambled out of the hole, grabbed the loud drum (Madong), and began banging it with all his might. Then he ran away as fast as he could.

Hearing the sound of the Madong, (drum) the villagers came running, thinking they had finally caught Kummtibaa. But when they reached the spot, they were shocked. It wasn't Kummtibaa caught in the trap it was the poor old Chokidar! Once again, Kummtibaa had outsmarted them, leaving the villagers with nothing but regret and frustration.

chapter four
Stars in day

Chapter Four

Stars in Day

Once upon a time, a special Mishmi ritual puja was organized in a village nestled in the hills. Many villagers were excited to attend, each carrying beautiful jewelry and gifts to offer to the hosts. The journey to the puja was not easy the path was steep and winding but everyone was cheerful chatting and laughing as they walked.

As they traveled, they talked about Kummtibaa a clever trickster known for his cunning ways." He's so sly He can fool anyone," one villager said. Another chimed in, "But 'I'm cleverer than Kummtibaa He could never trick me!" The group laughed and agreed saying "Yes, we're all too clever for Kummtibaa."

Little did they know, Kummtibaa was walking among them listening to their boasts. Hearing them challenge his cleverness made him feel angry, but also excited.

Suddenly he exclaimed, "I'm Kummtibaa and yes, I can fool you all" The villagers were shocked and shouted back, "Oh, so you're the cunning one! But you can't fool us!"

Kummtibaa smiled to himself, knowing he had a plan. "If I can trick you, you must give me all your jewelry," he declared. The villagers filled with confidence, laughed and agreed saying "Go ahead, We're not afraid!"

Kummtibaa walked silently letting the chatter continue around him. As they hiked, the villagers began to wonder if Kummtibaa had given up since, he hadn't tried to trick them yet. Maybe he knows he can't fool us they thought feeling proud of their cleverness.

Suddenly, Kummtibaa picked up the pace racing ahead until, he reached a clearing at the top of the hill. He stood there gazing up at the sky with a serious expression. When the villagers caught up they asked curiously "kummtibaa why are you staring at the sky?"

"Look everyone!" Kummtibaa pointed. There are so many stars shining brightly today! The villagers looked up to the sky puzzled.

"Where? Where are the stars? It's daytime!"

Just then a shower of sparkly jewelry fell from the villagers tokaris (basket) as they looked up at the sky. "The jewelry scattered all around them and kummtibaa laughed" The villagers gasped in shock realizing they had been tricked. Kummtibaa laughed saying see? "I fooled you Now according to our deal you must give me all your jewelry"

The villagers feeling upset and defeated, had to hand over their treasures. Kummtibaa was delighted with his victory. With a spring in his step, he walked away from the village, leaving the villagers to wonder how they had been so easily fooled.

And Kummtibaa the trickster claimed his prize and the villagers learned a valuable lesson.

chapter five
The trick on the hanging bridge.

The Trick on the Hanging Bridge

In the Mishmi community, there was one name that everyone whispered about with anger and frustration 'kummtibaa'. Known far and wide for his cunning tricks, he deceived countless innocent villagers. People were furious with him, but back in those days without the internet, no one knew what Kummtibaa actually looked like. This anonymity allowed him to keep tricking people without getting caught until one fateful day.

Kummtibaa was caught red handed, trying to steal food from the village storeroom. Enraged, the villagers finally had enough.

They dragged him to the old hanging bridge, tied him up tightly, and left him there, hoping he would learn a lesson for all his misdeeds.

At that time, an eye disease was spreading through the village. Many people were suffering from sore, swollen eyes, unsure of how to cure it.

As luck would have it, one unsuspecting villager was crossing the hanging bridge when he noticed Kummtibaa tied up.

"Hey, why are you tied up here on this bridge?" the man asked curiously, completely unaware that he was speaking to the notorious trickster himself.

Thinking quickly, Kummtibaa saw a chance to save himself. With a clever smile, he answered "Ah good sir, this is actually a special therapy for eye problems! I had terrible eye pain, but after three days of hanging here, my eyes feel perfectly fine. Today's my last day of the cure."

The man's eyes filled with hope. "Really? My eyes hurt too, and so do many people's back in my village Would you teach me this therapy?"

Kummtibaa grinned inwardly, realizing

he'd found another fool to trick. "Of course!"

All you have to do is untie me, and

I'll gladly show you how to do it.

Excited, the man quickly freed Kummtibaa. then kummtibaa tied him up and said to him "Now, close your eyes tightly its a crucial part of the therapy."

The man obediently shut his eyes, waiting for the promised miracle cure. But the moment his eyes were closed, Kummtibaa took off as fast as he could, disappearing down the road. After a few seconds, the man opened his eyes, looking around in confusion.

"Wait a minute ! where did he go? Realization dawned on him. "Oh no! I got tricked by Kummtibaa!"

chapter six
KUMMTIBAA'S LAST CLEVER TRICK.

Chapter Six

Kummtibaa's Last Clever Trick

Kummtibaa, known far and wide for his clever tricks and relentless cunning had a reputation for mischief was so infamous that, even on his final day, he couldn't resist deceiving others. In those days, food was scarce in the village. Families had to be careful to save what little they had, especially for their children.

But Kummtibaa was both greedy and shameless. He regularly snuck into homes, stealing the food that parents had carefully stored for their children. The villagers were frustrated, their children were left starving and crying, while Kummtibaa continued his sneaky thievery without a trace of regret.

Finally, the village chief had enough. "This has gone too far, he declared. "Kummtibaa is making our lives miserable. He has to be stopped". The villagers all agreed, shouting, "You're right" therefore, they devised a plan to put an end to his tricks once and for all.

The plan was simple. They would set out food laced with poison, hoping to catch Kummtibaa in the act. The villagers intentionally placed the food in a spot he was know to target, and then went about their day, warning their children not to touch it. The trap was set.

Sure enough that day, Kummtibaa sneaked into the village and spotted the food. Without a second thought, he devoured it.

But after a few minutes, he felt something strange, a sickness creeping through his body. His clever mind quickly realized what had happened. "They've poisoned me!" He thought, panic was rising.

In desperation, Kummtibaa scrambled up into the kaarong, a small low space between the ceiling and the roof where the Mishmi people keep things. He lay there, hoping to hide from the effects of the poison. But within an hour Kummtibaa took his last breath, and his tricks were finally over.

When the villagers returned, they searched everywhere for Kummtibaa, wondering where he could have gone. They couldn't find his body and began to believe that Kummtibaa was so strong that even poison couldn't kill him!

One of the villagers frustrated and doubting the poison's strength, decided to try a bit of the food himself. Sadly within an hour, he too lost his life.

The villagers gathered, murmuring to one another now convinced that Kummtibaa wasn't just clever but also strangely strong. Days passed and then, a foul smell began to spread from one of the houses. Insects dropped from the kaarong.

Therefore the homeowner climbed up to investigate. To his shock there lay kummtibaa's death body. 'ayooooooo!' he shouted. 'Kummtibaa isn't alive he's dead right here in my kaarong ! And all this time, we thought he'd escaped from our plan' The other villagers rushed over, starting in amazement. 'What a tricksters this man was,' they said, shaking heads. **'He fooled us all even on his death.' And so, Kummtibaa's legend lived on as the man whose cunning never left him, even in his final moments.**

REAL PICTURES EVIDENCE OF KUMMTIBAA CUNNING TRICKS

"Even today, the giant rock remains as proof of Kummtibaa's trickery, reminding all of the tale passed down through generations."